It is a Fox

Written by Alison Milford

Collins

Look! It is a red fox.

big tail

3

Look! It has a deep den in the woods.

cubs

Look! This fox has a thick fur coat.

fur footpads

Look! It is a fennec fox.

short legs

Look! It is a wood fox.

sharp teeth

Look! This fox can hear rabbits.

big bat ears

Look at the fox!

After reading

Letters and Sounds: Phase 3

Word count: 57

Focus phonemes: /ai/ /ee/ /oa/ /oo/ /ur/ /ear/ /ar/ /or/ bb, nn

Common exception word: the

Curriculum links: Understanding the World, People and communities: make observations of animals

Early learning goals: Reading: use phonic knowledge to decode regular words and read them aloud accurately

Developing fluency

- Your child may enjoy hearing you read the book.
- Ask your child to choose a spread from the book. Model reading, **Look!**, with lots of expression. Now ask your child to do the same and to read the rest of the text on the page with the same expression.

Phonic practice

- Practise reading words with long vowel sounds together. Look at the word **ears** on page 13. Ask your child to sound talk and blend the letter sounds ear/s.
- Can they find another word with the long vowel sound /ear/ in this spread? (*hear*) Ask them to sound talk and blend it.

Extending vocabulary

- Ask your child to find examples of adjectives in the book. Look for all the words that describe different parts of foxes e.g. *red*, *thick* (fur), *sharp* (teeth), *short* (legs).
- Look at the photo on pages 2 to 3 (or another photo, if your child would prefer). Can your child think of any other words to describe this fox?